Settling and UNSETTLING the West

Katelyn Rice

Consultants

Vanessa Ann Gunther, Ph.D.
Department of History
Chapman University

Nicholas Baker, Ed.D.
Supervisor of Curriculum and Instruction
Colonial School District, DE

Katie Blomquist, Ed.S.
Fairfax County Public Schools

Publishing Credits

Rachelle Cracchiolo, M.S.Ed., *Publisher*
Conni Medina, M.A.Ed., *Managing Editor*
Emily R. Smith, M.A.Ed., *Series Developer*
Diana Kenney, M.A.Ed., NBCT, *Content Director*
Courtney Patterson, *Senior Graphic Designer*
Lynette Ordoñez, *Editor*

Image Credits: Cover and pp. 1, 8 (top), 17 (bottom), 23 (top), 25 (top), 27 (front) North Wind Picture Archives; p. 4 Pictorial Parade/Getty Images; p. 5 (top) Washington University, St. Louis, USA/Bridgeman Images, (left) Courtesy of UC Berkeley, Bancroft Library; pp. 5 (right), 31 Kansas State Historical Society; pp. 6, 9, 24-25 Granger, NYC; pp. 28-29 Sarin Images/Granger, NYC; pp. 6-7 Courtesy of the Montana Historical Society, X1952.01.10; p. 7 Public Domain; p. 8 (bottom) NARA [6883912]; p. 10 Ann Ronan Picture Library Heritage Images/Newscom; p. 11 Clark Kelley Price; p. 13 (top back) MPI/Getty Images, (top front) NARA [299808]; p. 13 (bottom) Whitman Mission National Historic Site, National Park Service; p. 15 (bottom) Peter Newark Pictures/Bridgeman Images, (middle) NARA [299809]; p. 17 (middle) Beinecke Rare Book and Manuscript Library Digital Collections; p. 18 (top) Peter Newark Western Americana/Bridgeman Images, (bottom right) LOC [LC-DIG-cwpbh-01671]; p. 20 (top) National Archives, General Records of the U.S. Government, (middle) Courtesy of the Rare Book Division of the Library of Congress, (bottom) University of Oklahoma Libraries Western History Collections; p. 21 Look and Learn/Bridgeman Images; pp. 23 (left), 26-27 Peter Newark Western Americana/Bridgeman Images; p. 23 (bottom) Bridgeman Images; p. 28 LOC [rbpe.01701000]; p. 29 (left) LOC [rbpe.07204800], (right) LOC [LC-DIG-pga-01416]; p. 32 NARA [6883912]; back cover Courtesy of UC Berkeley, Bancroft Library; all other images from iStock and/or Shutterstock.

Library of Congress Cataloging-in-Publication Data

Names: Rice, Katelyn.
Title: Settling and unsettling the West / Katelyn Rice.
Description: Huntington Beach, CA : Teacher Created Materials, [2017] | Includes index. | Audience: Grades 4-6.
Identifiers: LCCN 2016034141 (print) | LCCN 2016048209 (ebook) | ISBN 9781493837977 (pbk.) | ISBN 9781480757622 (eBook)
Subjects: LCSH: Pioneers--West (U.S.)--History--19th century--Juvenile literature. | Frontier and pioneer life--West (U.S.)--Juvenile literature.
| West (U.S.)--History--19th century--Juvenile literature.
Classification: LCC F596 .R526 2017 (print) | LCC F596 (ebook) | DDC 978/.02--dc23
LC record available at https://lccn.loc.gov/2016034141

Teacher Created Materials

5301 Oceanus Drive
Huntington Beach, CA 92649-1030
http://www.tcmpub.com

ISBN 978-1-4938-3797-7

© 2017 Teacher Created Materials, Inc.

Table of Contents

Welcome to the 1800s

The 1800s were a time of growth for the United States. The long fight for independence from Great Britain had come to an end. Now, people were looking to explore their new country. They were ready for adventure. The West was that adventure.

Life on the **frontier** was exciting. Rumors of gold gave hope to many. The promise of land and good farming drew people, too. The West was full of possibility.

But, the growth of the country also caused problems. As settlers moved westward, they pushed American Indians and Mexicans out of their homes.

The 1800s were a time of westward expansion. These settlers paved the way for the future of the United States.

People travel west in covered wagons.

Famous frontiersman Daniel Boone leads a group of settlers to Kentucky.

These ads encouraged people to settle in the West.

Why Move West?

A writer named John O'Sullivan had a huge impact on how people viewed the frontier. O'Sullivan was a smart man. He graduated college when he was just 18 years old. People always wanted to hear what he had to say. So, he started writing his ideas. In 1845, he published an article for a magazine. In it, he said that all of North America should be part of the United States. He said Americans were destined by God to own the land. This idea became know as **Manifest Destiny**. Many people liked this idea. They used it to justify the growth of the nation.

John O'Sullivan

Not everyone agreed with O'Sullivan. They argued that other people already lived in the West. American Indians had been living there for thousands of years. They did not think people had the right to take land from these **tribes**. Still, the idea of Manifest Destiny spread. And so did the nation's borders.

In this 1839 article, O'Sullivan describes the idea of Manifest Destiny before he coined the term.

a crowded apartment building in New York City in the late 1800s

LINCOLN'S BARGAIN

★★★★★

In 1862, President Abraham Lincoln signed the **Homestead** Act. It gave settlers land in the West if they farmed it and built a house there. After five years, the land would belong to them. This convinced many people to move west.

a Worchester, Massachusetts, factory in 1855

People headed west for many reasons. Some left their homes because of **push factors**. They hoped the West would help them start a new life. Life in the East was cramped. Big families lived together in small apartments. Factories and tall buildings crowded the streets. These factories were not safe places to work. Men and women worked for 12 hours or more every day and earned very little pay. Some children even worked in factories! They had to help their families earn money.

The Civil War was another push factor. It was fought over slavery and states' rights. Much of the South was destroyed after the war ended in 1865. People looked west for a fresh start.

Others headed west because of **pull factors**. Gold and silver were found in several places in the West. Gold and silver rushes soon followed. People flocked to the West in hopes of striking it rich. Land there was cheap and good for farming. Some people felt **oppressed** where they were. The West offered a chance at freedom. For some, that was worth risking it all.

Heading West

When people traveled west, they usually took their whole family. They went in covered wagons that were pulled by horses, mules, or oxen. Wagons were big, but people still had to leave most of their things behind. Some people even traveled on foot for thousands of miles so they could fit more items into the wagon.

Timing was important when heading west. If travelers left too early, there would be no grass along the trail for their animals to eat. If they left too late, they might get caught in heavy snow. They had to leave at just the right time.

Settlers struggle to get their wagon across a snowy bridge.

ALL ABOUT WAGONS

★★★★★★★

Wagons were made of wood and had white fabric over the top for protection from the weather. They were 12 feet (3.6 meters) long with wheels that were 6 ft. (1.8 m) tall. People often traveled in long lines called *wagon trains* for safety.

A family buries a loved one along the trail.

Even if settlers found the perfect time to leave, traveling on the trails was still hard. A lot could happen to a person along the way. Some people were run over by wagons. Wild weather could cause wagons to break or get stuck. And sometimes, animals trampled travelers. But, disease was by far the biggest killer. For every mile of the trail, between 10 and 15 people died from disease. Those who died were buried in shallow graves along the trail.

Even with all of these dangers, people still headed west. Their journeys made trails that led from one side of the country to the other.

The Oregon Trail

One of the first routes traveled was the Oregon Trail. Traders and fur trappers blazed the trail in 1811. By the 1830s, it was being used by settlers in covered wagons, too. The trail started in Missouri and ended in Oregon. That's 2,170 miles (3,492 kilometers)! The trip could take up to six months. But, it was better than traveling by sea. That took a year or longer.

Many settlers thought the long trip to Oregon would be worth the journey. Reports of **fertile** land promised good farming. And land was cheap enough for people to start a new life. But, there was a problem. Great Britain had already claimed much of this area. The United States and Great Britain tried to rule the territory together. But as more people came to Oregon, arguments began.

Great Britain and the United States couldn't decide who owned the land. In 1846, the two sides came to an agreement. They split the area in half. The United States took the south and Great Britain took the north. The deal added 286,000 square mi. (741,000 square km) to the United States. The young country was growing quickly.

disputed Oregon Territory

Oregon Trail

The Oregon Treaty created a boundary between the United States and the land we now know as Canada.

MEET THE WHITMANS

Marcus and Narcissa Whitman were two **emigrants**. Narcissa wrote about what she saw along the Oregon Trail. Her letters were published and became very popular. People wanted to read about life on the frontier.

The Santa Fe Trail

Ten years after people began using the Oregon Trail, a trader named William Becknell started another trail. The Santa Fe Trail also began in Missouri. But, it went south and ended in New Mexico. It soon became a **trade route** across the United States. Settlers traded fur from the West for goods from the East. As more people arrived, the trail was used to deliver mail. Settlers sent letters home about finding silver. Soon, more and more people arrived hoping to get rich.

Not everyone was happy with the new settlers. The United States had **annexed** Texas in 1845. But, the western border wasn't clear. Settlers were claiming land that Mexicans said belonged to them. In 1846, the first shots of the Mexican-American War were fired. Both sides fought hard for two years. Then, in 1848, the United States and Mexico signed a **treaty**. The treaty sold over half of Mexico to the United States! The United States paid just $15 million for the land. This new territory drew more people to the Southwest. The Santa Fe Trail was the best way to get there.

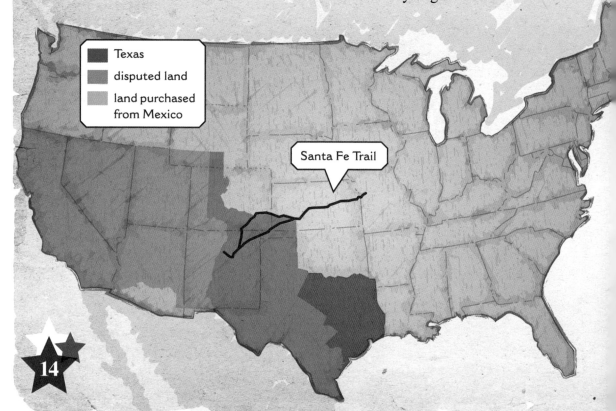

- Texas
- disputed land
- land purchased from Mexico

Santa Fe Trail

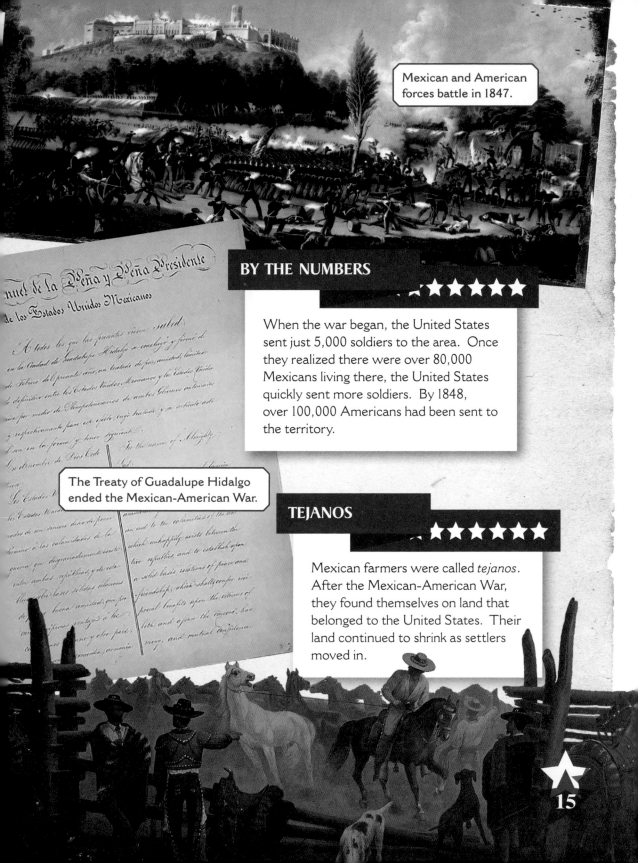

Mexican and American forces battle in 1847.

BY THE NUMBERS

★★★★★★

When the war began, the United States sent just 5,000 soldiers to the area. Once they realized there were over 80,000 Mexicans living there, the United States quickly sent more soldiers. By 1848, over 100,000 Americans had been sent to the territory.

The Treaty of Guadalupe Hidalgo ended the Mexican-American War.

TEJANOS

★★★★★★

Mexican farmers were called *tejanos*. After the Mexican-American War, they found themselves on land that belonged to the United States. Their land continued to shrink as settlers moved in.

The California Trail

The California Trail opened in 1841. It wasn't popular at first. The trail was dangerous. The route began along the Oregon Trail. But, near Idaho, the two trails split. If travelers wanted to go north, they took the Oregon Trail. Going south took them along the California Trail. After the split, people had to travel through deserts in Utah and Nevada. Then, they had to cross the Sierra Nevada Mountains. It has some of the tallest mountains in the country! It took months to cross the Sierras. Getting caught in the snow had deadly consequences. Even with the dangers of the trail, people were still willing to try.

In 1848, James Marshall discovered gold in California. News spread across the country. Many people thought they could get rich quick. By the next year, 80,000 people had moved to California. They were called 49ers. Many of them had used the California and Oregon trails. Over the next 5 years, more than 250,000 people made the dangerous journey. Some traveled all the way from Europe! Slowly, the gold ran out and the California Gold Rush came to an end. Yet many people stayed.

California Trail

Sierra Nevada mountain range

THE CALIFORNIA HERALD.

This 1848 newspaper describes the discovery of gold in California.

49ERS

★★★★★★★

Many **pioneers** headed to California when news spread that gold had been discovered. By the time most of them had arrived, it was 1849. Americans began referring to these gold-seeking pioneers as 49ers and the name stuck.

A 49er pans for gold in California.

Mormon pioneers journey to Salt Lake City.

Joseph Smith

Brigham Young

The Mormon Trail

When Joseph Smith founded the **Mormon** religion in 1830, it grew quickly. But, many people did not like the new religion. They didn't like that Mormons practiced **polygamy**. And the quick spread of the new religion scared many people. They burned Mormon homes and farms. In 1846, Smith was killed by an angry mob. After that, many Mormons decided it was time to move. They wanted to go west. The route they took is known as the Mormon Trail.

Brigham Young became the leader of the Mormon religion after Smith. He led 3,000 people west in February of 1846. They hoped to make it to Utah before the next winter came. But it was still very cold. There was too much ice and snow for them to travel safely. So, they decided to stop at the Missouri River for a few months. On July 24, 1847, the first group of Mormons arrived in Salt Lake City, Utah. They had left their homes more than a year before. Over the next 20 years, nearly 70,000 Mormons crossed the Mormon Trail.

As more settlers headed west, the United States continued to expand. The young country was growing in size and strength. But, this fast growth caused problems with the people already living there.

Mormon Trail

Unsettling the West

Not everyone was pleased that people were moving west. American Indians had been living on the land for thousands of years. As settlers moved, they wanted more and more land. They thought it was their destiny. So, they kicked American Indians out. As the country grew, tribes lost millions of acres.

In 1830, President Andrew Jackson signed the Indian Removal Act. It made Eastern tribes move west of the Mississippi River. Now, they had to live on land called **reservations**. Once they were there, they were not allowed to leave. Over the next 20 years, nearly 100,000 American Indians were forced to move west. And more settlers kept coming. The United States took more and more tribal land. They forced tribes to stay in smaller and smaller areas. Many tribes decided to fight back.

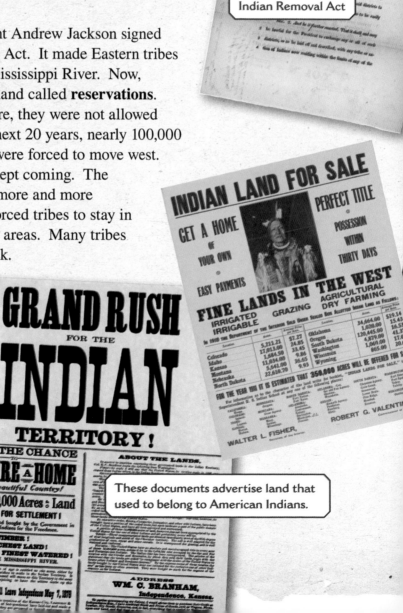

Indian Removal Act

These documents advertise land that used to belong to American Indians.

American Indians walk the Trail of Tears.

TRAIL OF TEARS

★★★★★★★★

The Cherokee tribe was forced to walk 800 mi. (1,300 km) to their new reservations. Almost one-third of the original 15,000 died from hunger or disease along the way. This walk became known as the Trail of Tears.

Many battles were fought between the U.S. government and the tribes. Some were fought when people refused to leave their homes. That was the case with the three Seminole Wars. The Seminole tribe refused to leave Florida and live on reservations. When soldiers arrived, the people fought back. But they were outnumbered. By 1858, almost all Seminoles had left Florida.

Other wars were fought when settlers tried to take over American Indian land. Red Cloud was a Lakota war chief. When gold was discovered in Montana in 1863, the government tried to set up a trail through his tribe's land. So, the tribe fought back. After two years, the government withdrew. They agreed that the Lakota owned the land. But peace did not last long.

In 1874, gold was again found on Lakota land. The government tried to force the Lakota to move. When the tribe refused, General Custer came up with a plan. On June 25, 1876, he attacked the tribe in what became known as the Battle of the Little Bighorn. But, Custer's soldiers were outnumbered and unprepared. He and all his men were killed. After that, U.S. troops swarmed the region and sent the tribe to a reservation.

A FAMILY AFFAIR ★★★★★★

George Armstrong Custer and four members of his family were killed at the Battle of the Little Bighorn. Today, the Battle of the Little Bighorn is also called Custer's Last Stand.

U.S. soldiers capture Seminole chiefs.

Chief Red Cloud

Battle of the Little Bighorn

23

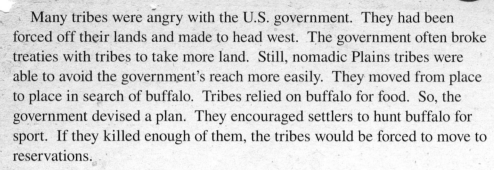

Many tribes were angry with the U.S. government. They had been forced off their lands and made to head west. The government often broke treaties with tribes to take more land. Still, nomadic Plains tribes were able to avoid the government's reach more easily. They moved from place to place in search of buffalo. Tribes relied on buffalo for food. So, the government devised a plan. They encouraged settlers to hunt buffalo for sport. If they killed enough of them, the tribes would be forced to move to reservations.

Tribes only killed what they needed. But, settlers killed many more. Sometimes, they took buffalo hides and sold them. Other times, they just left the dead buffalo along the trails. In 1800, there were over 80 million buffalo living in the United States. By 1900, there were only 500 left. Because of this tactic, buffalo almost went extinct. Many tribes suffered. They joined other tribes on reservations. Settlers rushed to claim the new land in the name of destiny.

Americans shoot buffalo from a train.

American Indian camp in 1848

A Growing Nation

The 1800s were a time of growth for the United States. As more people moved west, travel changed. Trails were cleared and new routes were discovered. In 1869, the first railroad to stretch from the East to the West was completed. This made travel much faster and safer. The trails were used less and less. **Settlements** sprang up along the railroads. People settled into their new homes in the West. The possibilities seemed endless.

The transcontinental railroad passes through a small town in the 1800s.

But, the settling of the West also caused many problems. The United States was at odds with Great Britain yet again. And, a war with Mexico left Mexicans angry at the United States. These feelings would take many years to fade. American Indians lost their homes when they were forced to move. And the buffalo population was almost completely wiped out.

The new country explored its borders in the 1800s. Twenty-eight new states were added. Suddenly, the United States was one of the largest countries in the world. And it was still growing.

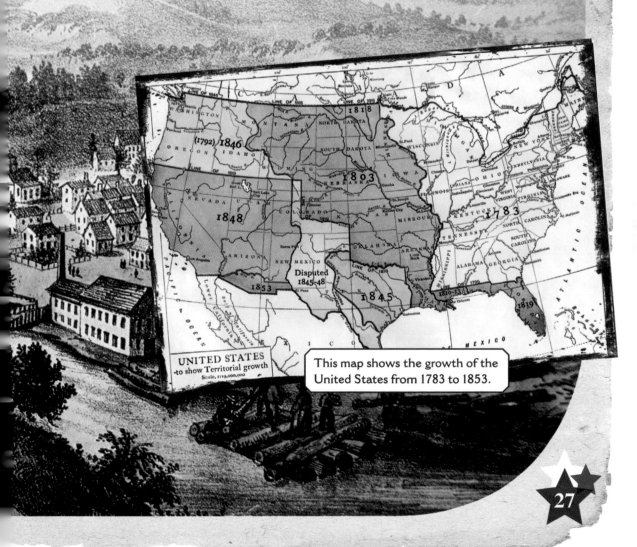

This map shows the growth of the United States from 1783 to 1853.

Advertise It!

Getting what you needed to survive on the frontier wasn't always easy. There were few stores in the West. Storeowners had to carry many products for their customers. Frontier stores often sold everything from food to medicine to wagon parts.

Imagine you are a storeowner on the frontier. What will you stock? What might pioneers need that they can't get on their own? Create an advertisement for your store. Include popular items and drawings of what your store carries. Then, give your store a catchy name. Share your poster with friends and family members.

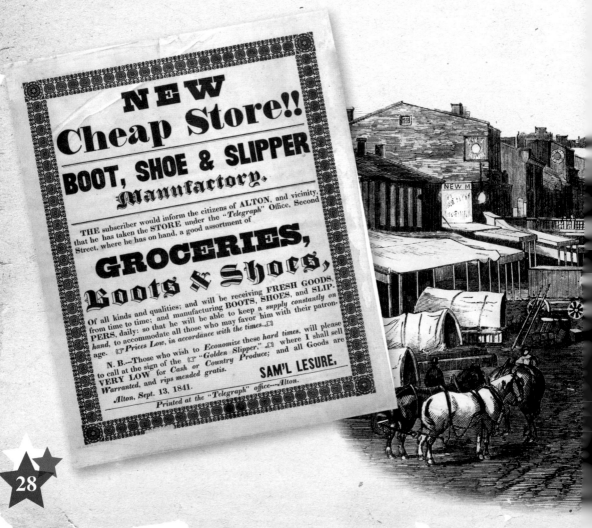

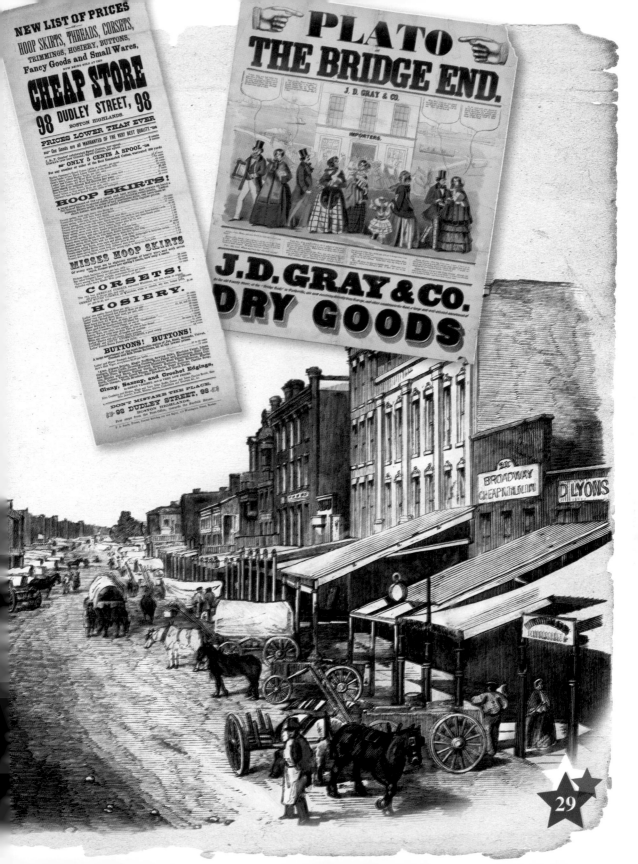

Glossary

annexed—added a territory or place to a country

emigrants—people who leave a country or region to live elsewhere

fertile—capable of supporting the growth of many plants

frontier—an area where few people live

homestead—land people acquired from the government by farming and living on it

Manifest Destiny—the idea that the United States had a right to extend its borders to the Pacific Ocean

Mormon—a member of a Christian church founded by Joseph Smith

oppressed—treated a person or group of people in a cruel or unfair way

pioneers—people who are the first to explore and settle a new place

polygamy—the act of being married to more than one person at the same time

pull factors—the advantages of a place that make people want to move there

push factors—the disadvantages of a place that make people want to move away

reservations—areas of land in the United States for American Indians to live

settlements—places where people have come to live and where few people lived before

trade route—a course followed by traders and merchants

treaty—a formal agreement made between two or more countries or groups

tribes—groups of people who have the same language, customs, and beliefs

Index

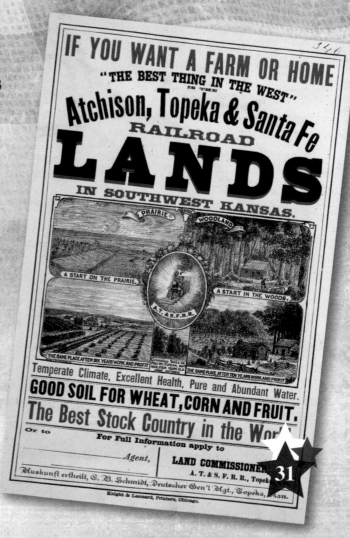

Your Turn!

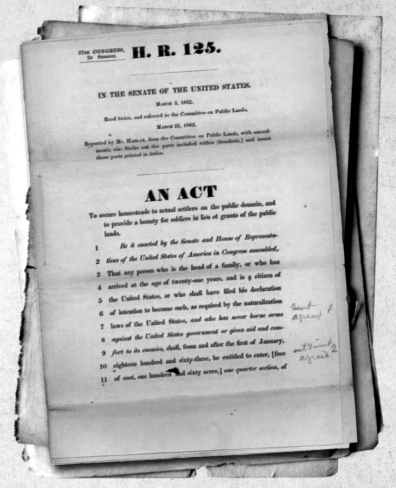

Stay or Go?

The Homestead Act was a major pull factor in the 1800s. It encouraged many people to settle the frontier. Moving west was not easy, though. And once settlers arrived, they had to start new lives. Write a list of pros and cons that settlers might have considered when making the decision to move west.